THEY DIED TOO YOUNG

BUDDY HOLLY

by
Tom Stockdale

This edition first published by Parragon Books Ltd in 1995

Produced by
Magpie Books Ltd, London

Copyright © Parragon Book Service Ltd 1995
Unit 13–17, Avonbridge Trading Estate
Atlantic Road
Avonmouth
Bristol BS11 9QD

Illustrations courtesy of: Rex Features; Associated Press.

ISBN 0 75250 675 7

A copy of the British Library Cataloguing in Publication
Data is available from the British Library.

Typeset by Hewer Text Composition Services, Edinburgh
Printed in Singapore by Printlink International Co.

Buddy Holly's professional recording career covered less than three years, from 1956 to the beginning of 1959, but during that time he set standards at the time of the irresistible rise of rock 'n' roll, providing an influence which the rock world has acknowledged to this day. His guitar playing brought country and rhythm & blues styles together in a new form which had instant appeal, and the extent to which his songs have been covered by other artists is evidence of their effect. The short time which he had to establish such a hold can be equalled by Jimi Hendrix, but by the time Hendrix came into the spotlight, Holly had been dead for over six years, and had already changed the rock idiom to the benefit of every musician who came after him. He was one of the first white rock stars to use his own material, and the Crickets were the first white band to use the now standard four-piece line-up. And Holly was free of the less savoury influences with which Hendrix lived and died – a 'nice guy and first rate performer' as one DJ described him. He cut a vinyl legacy by sheer confidence and innovation, at a time when rock may still have been in its infancy, but was already taking its first steps.

Quiet Beginnings

Charles Hardin Holley was born on 7 September, 1936, in Lubbock, Texas. (The more familiar 'Holly' spelling is the result of a mistake on Buddy's first recording contract.) He was the youngest of Lawrence and Ella Holley's four children, and was raised like the rest of the family as a Fundamentalist Baptist, in the strict moral atmosphere of the Bible belt of south-west America. His father had moved to

Lubbock in search of work in the thriving cotton industry of the area, and although Texas was not especially known for its musical heritage, his family made music a part of their lives. From the singing which was an important part of their church life, to the music which they played and sang at home, Buddy, as he was called from an early age, was surrounded by its influence. He won a five-dollar prize at the age of 5, with a rendition of *Down The River Of Memories*, accompanying himself on a toy violin. He was keen to follow his brothers and sister by mastering an instrument, trying the piano and the steel guitar before finding an affinity with the acoustic guitar, listening to the radio and picking up the tunes of the day. He was an easy-going child, but obstinate, and once he had decided to take the instrument seriously there was no way he wasn't going to take it beyond a certain level. As a student at school he was adequate, but did not shine in anything; his personality comes through in a comment from a teacher made after Buddy's death, that 'it was only after the news in the papers about his death that I remembered that he had been in my class. He was a quiet kid – wasn't any great student, but didn't cause any trouble either. So I really don't remember anything about him.'

In 1949, Buddy and his new friend Bob Montgomery started to play together, mostly the traditional country music of the region. Hank Williams was an early favourite, whose musical legacy was the breaking of the traditional style of country music – by including elements of rockabilly – before his alcohol-induced death in December 1952. By 1953 Buddy and Bob were playing as a duo at every available opportunity, gaining a regular spot on a local radio station with their self-styled 'Western and Bop'. Although Buddy had other interests, including hunting, fishing, leatherwork, reading and painting, the music had taken hold of him, and his ambition simply to make a living from it gave no indication of the way he would change the industry in which he chose to work. As a part of a sophomore English class Buddy wrote: 'My life has been what you might call an uneventful one, and it seems there is not much of interest to tell . . . I have thought about making a career out of Western music if I am good enough, but I will just have to wait to see how that turns out . . . '

By that time, America had settled into its post-war attitude of growth and change, and discontented young people had discovered the vitality of music coming from the small local black radio stations. From the roots of blues and jazz, and the influence of gospel music, names like Ray Charles and Fats Domino joined the blues sounds of Howlin' Wolf and Muddy Waters and became a revelation for anyone wanting more than what Frank Sinatra and Bing Crosby had to offer. For the white-dominated record industry it would take the appearance of a Bill Haley or an Elvis Presley for this black style to take off with the white majority, and it is only the name rock 'n' roll that began in the early 1950s; the actual music had been there to be listened to and danced to for some years.

The Three Tunes To The Crickets

In 1953 Buddy and Bob got together with a contemporary of theirs, Larry Welborn, who played the bass, and Buddy became more interested in the R&B that was coming over the airwaves. He had a steady girlfriend, called Echo, but even she had to take third place in his life behind music and cars – his regular speeding caused him to lose his licence for a while. The trio travelled 200 miles to make a demo tape in Wichita Falls, but nothing came of it and they continued to play local gigs, recording primitive songs at home. Bob was the main songwriter of the band, although Buddy's mother participated in some of the writing – both his parents gave him their full support.

The Buddy, Bob and Larry Trio kicked off at a Lubbock gig headlined by Bill Haley and The Comets on 14 October, 1955. Haley was in his first flush of fame after the hit 'Rock Around The Clock', and film of the time still conveys the excitement that the new sound caused. The next day, they witnessed the charged atmosphere around the up-and-coming

Buddy Holly

The blues sounds of Ray Charles were an
inspiration to Buddy Holly

'Hillbilly Cat', as Elvis Presley was called, opening for him at a concert in Lubbock. It is likely that the wild reaction to Presley had a hand in the frenetic style that Holly developed on stage, despite the high school-looking promotion shots that we associate with him. The death of James Dean in September 1955 had turned rebellion into a necessity for the youth of America, and rock 'n' roll dancing was a natural way for Dean's direction-less anger to be copied, away from the Slim Whitman and Tony Bennett songs that still dominated the charts. The shocked older generation was concerned at the antics of the overtly sexual beat, and the explicit immorality of musicians like Jerry Lee Lewis and Little Richard made their music a thing to be banned in many homes. Buddy's upbringing kept him at a distance from the more 'dangerous' aspects of the music, but he became hooked on the beat, and the fact that Elvis used a drummer meant that it wasn't long before Buddy, Bob and Larry soon brought Jerry Allison into the band to fulfil that role.

Bill Haley's booking agent, Eddie Crandell approached several record companies on behalf of Buddy, Bob and Larry, and Decca offered a trial, but they only wanted one vocalist. Bob persuaded Buddy to take on that role as, where Bob was more keen to follow a country bias, Buddy was a confirmed rock 'n' roller, and Decca were looking to build on their rock 'n' roll stable, led by Bill Haley. Larry and Jerry, who were 17 (Buddy and Bob were 19), could not get time off school for the trip to Nashville, so Buddy took bassist Don Guess and guitarist Sonny Curtis, with whom he had played before. With producer Owen Bradley, they recorded four tracks on 26 January, 1956, and the single 'Blue Days–Black Nights/Love Me' was released during April. It failed to make a mark, although Gene Vincent, who was recording at the studio, thought it was a great record.

The band continued playing, calling themselves Buddy Holly and The Three Tunes, and playing exclusively rock 'n' roll, with Buddy using one of Leo Fender's recently produced Fender Stratocaster guitars, a sight that would, along with his subsequent change from metal to black-rimmed glasses, set his image for the future. The dances that they played proved the potency of the solid rhythm that the country was going wild over; that year, Elvis was watched by an estimated 50 million on the *Ed Sullivan Show*. A number of demos were produced by The Three Tunes, some original, like 'Because I Love You' and 'Rock-A-Bye-Rock', some covers of Elvis, Fats Domino, Chuck Berry and Bo Diddley. After Buddy's death, these would become the major reservoir for Holly releases. They suggest a rapid progression from stylized copies of their originals, to Buddy's discovery of a personal style which would prove its success in only a matter of months.

Another Decca session six months later produced five more tracks, including a version of 'That'll Be The Day', which Bradley hated – apparently, Holly hit him in the face! The resulting single, 'Modern Don Juan/You Are My One Desire' brought as little success as the first attempt. In between the sessions the band struggled to make a living by opening for the groups that played in Lubbock, and doing several small tours around the area. Their local radio contacts were important for the dance bookings that were vital for profile-raising, as well as for the modest fees on which they had to survive. Buddy's insistence on buying the best equipment available is proof of his seriousness, but left him with a hefty debt to his brother and a need to play wherever and whenever he could. A third visit to Nashville, using session players, didn't impress Decca enough, so early in 1957 Buddy was looking for another deal. He was, however, confident that he was heading in the right direction; the evidence of ten Elvis singles in the American top 100 at the end of 1956 was proof of the potency of the new music.

He was also looking for new musicians, for only Jerry Allison had stayed the course. The two still performed regularly, creating what friends remembered as an impressive skeletal duo, with the primitive, basic rhythms that would carry over into the full group. Buddy's guitar technique grew with the need for him to supply all the music, and Allison would later say that 'I haven't played with anyone since, that I could play with as well'.

On 25 February, 1957 Buddy recalled Larry Welborn and added guitarist Niki Sullivan, in a trip to the nearest available recording studio, in Clovis, New Mexico. The NorVaJak Studio had been set up by musician Norman Petty for his own use, with the proceeds from several moderate hits by his Trio in the early 1950s. The relaxed nature of Petty's set-up provided a bonus for the penniless Three Tunes, in that Petty charged by results, rather than by the hour, and the

tiny studio had already proved a
success for Roy Orbison ('Ooby Doo-
by') and The Rhythm Orchids ('I'm
Stickin' With You' and 'Party Doll').
Buddy recorded 'That'll Be The Day'
and 'I'm Looking For Someone To
Love', although there was a problem
with the former, in that Decca still had
rights over it from the contract of the
previous year. They decided to hide
Buddy's name under the cover of a
new band; the resulting search through
an encyclopedia provided the name
that brought fame, The Crickets.
(The story of a buzzing noise in the
studio insulation that turned out to be
a noisy insect is a myth.) The relationship between Buddy and Petty
worked, and one of the most valuable
partnerships in rock 'n' roll began.

Bill Hayley

Rock 'n' roll was just taking off when Buddy
Holly arrived on the scene

Petty got involved in the band's management, and his previous recording
success came in handy for contacts in
record companies. Despite the excitement that rock 'n' roll was causing
around the country there were still
companies who refused to believe
that the music was worth investing
in; so several rejections had already
been received by the time Petty got
the tapes to Coral Records. Although
a subsidiary of Decca, Coral were
autonomous, and were keen enough
on the songs to release the single on 27
May 1957. During this time, Welborn
had to return to other musical com-
mitments, and he was replaced on the
bass with another Lubbock local, Joe B
Mauldin.

Progress was not swift for the single in America, but it was sure, and it made number 1 by the end of September. Buddy's bespectacled face was a reassuring alternative to the violent rebel image portrayed by Gene Vincent or Eddie Cochran, and it can be imagined that the softer nature of his lyrics got him past the parental bans that baulked against the streetwise cool of Cochran's 'Summertime Blues'. In Britain, reaction was ecstatic, and the single was at the top of the charts after three weeks, helped by the influence of the Alan Freed 'Disc Jockey Jamboree' show on Radio Luxembourg – required listening for young rock 'n' rollers. British youth was desperate for anything American in the mid-1950s, and 'That'll Be The

Day' overtook three Elvis singles and Jerry Lee Lewis' 'Whole Lotta Shakin' Goin' On' in the top 20 of November 1957.

The 21 year-old Holly's songwriting was by now as prolific as it was innovative, and the industry habit of releasing only four singles a year by any one group gave Petty the idea of releasing Buddy's material on a solo basis as well as with The Crickets. So, while Brunswick Records took over the band releases, Coral concentrated on Buddy Holly records, bringing out 'Words Of Love' in mid-1957, although not successfully. The song is notable, though, for Buddy's double-tracked vocals, a technique which is automatically used today, but which no one had thought of then, and which was only achieved at that time by singing the vocals with exact timing onto a separate tape recorder. He would also experiment with the technique on his guitar. The song was written, as were most of his others, as a whole – the words and music coming to Buddy at the same time. He didn't seem to need to hang around for the right lyric to fit a melody; the complete package suggested itself for him to present to the band.

Success And Independence

'That'll Be The Day' brought immediate star-status to The Crickets and they were booked on a four-month tour with the 'Biggest Show of Stars of '57'. The show was aptly named, with a billing that included Fats Domino, the Everly Brothers, Frankie Lymon and The Teenagers, Paul Anka, Chuck Berry, The Drifters, Jimmy Bowen, Clyde McPhatter and Lavern Baker. The 15-minute sets by each artist provided a procession of current hits for the crowds, during two exhausting shows each night, and there was not much rest on the uncomfortable coach trips to the next destination.

There was further discomfort caused by the continued colour-bar in some states. Earlier that year, Nat 'King' Cole had been beaten up on stage in Birmingham, Alabama. The black acts in the 'Stars of '57' would sometimes have to use a different hotel from the white ones, who were also stopped from playing some of the gigs. On one occasion the tour party was stopped by the police and ordered to segregate themselves into the two tour buses, making a particularly

The Crickets

The jukebox helped to spread the craze for rock 'n' roll

uncomfortable ride for the 90 per cent black contingent. British band-leader Ted Heath had returned from America saying 'Rock'n'roll is mainly performed by coloured artists for coloured people, and is therefore unlikely ever to prove popular in Britain'. The racism affected the tour party, although the music they all played helped to erode the differ-ences. Buddy apparently got thump-ed by Lavern Baker, but he got on well with Chuck Berry, and they would shoot craps together at the back of the coach. The thought of them chasing a stray dice under the seats of a bus is a happy one, bringing to mind that they were just a couple of young men on an adventure, in contrast to the image we have of them now as two of the giant influences of popular music.

The Crickets had put down a few tracks before they set off on the tour, to allow for new releases, and the thirteen numbers contained some nuggets. Of the eight tracks for Buddy's solo effort, the two highlights were 'Everyday' and 'Peggy Sue'. 'Everyday' was remarkable for its thigh-slapping drum part, recorded because Allison's drumming was too loud for the small Clovis studio. 'Peggy Sue' is classic Holly, and created a rock heroine in Buddy's shy, teenage style. The song was originally entitled 'Cindy Lou', but was renamed after Jerry Allison's fiancée. The five songs earmarked for Cricket release included 'Oh Boy!' and the Bo Diddley song 'Not Fade Away'. In a single year Buddy had recorded some of the most influential songs for the bands that would grow to prominence in the 1960s, and both The Beatles and The Rolling Stones would pay tribute to him in their early music. And 'Oh Boy!' gave its name and excitement to the television pop show that attracted the eyes and ears of a whole generation.

On one of the enforced bans during the tour, The Crickets took advantage of the break to record the final songs for a debut album. By its release in November 1957, both 'Peggy Sue' and 'Oh Boy!' had gone into the top ten in America; again, in Britain

the singles charted even more qui
and in 'Oh Boy!' 's case to an e
higher chart position than in Americ
reaching number 3. The band picture
on the sleeve of the album, *The
'Chirping' Crickets*, showed the effect
of a Niki Sullivan punch on Jerry
Allison's eye, but all Buddy's punches
were in the music. The album had all
the Holly hallmarks, and put him
firmly amongst those rock musicians
who sing about love, rather than sex.
His lyrics were playful and plaintive,
teasing and charming, and accompa-
nied by a sympathetic vocal style,
swooping between octaves, and with
its instantly identifiable voice-breaking
hiccup serenading the female youth of
the late 1950s.

er, the band had dis-
shirts and jeans for
.ch brought style into
ge, as they appeared on the
.ullivan Show. This was also around
.ne time that Buddy started to wear the
trademark black-rimmed glasses,
which no musician since has been
able to wear without some reference
being made to Buddy Holly. The
Lubbock Avalanche Journal announced
the television show with pride, add-
ing that 'they do their own playing
without orchestra assistance'! They
performed 'That'll Be The Day' and
'Peggy Sue', although apparently they
did not get on very well with Ed
himself, and after a second appearance
in January, Buddy refused to do the
show again.

Niki Sullivan decided to leave the band after the long tour; as a singer/ songwriter himself he probably needed some space to devote to his own career. He was definitely playing the supporting role to Buddy's guitar, as can be seen by the fact that Buddy decided to continue as a three-piece: himself, Jerry Allison and Joe Mauldin. This line-up took its place on another large bill, this time to play a dozen gigs over Christmas at one venue, the Paramount Theatre, in New York. Introduced by the self-proclaimed inventor of rock 'n' roll, Alan Freed, The Crickets joined Fats, Jerry Lee, the Everlys, the Rays, Danny and The Juniors, Paul Anka, The Teenagers (without Lymon) and more. There were up to six shows a day, but the lack of travelling made a big difference to their energy levels. On stage, Buddy was a different person from the mild-mannered man he was off it. The Paramount concerts were a typical example of his audience-rousing style. He was very keen to be the best at anything that he did, and the live shows got everybody dancing. 'He would tear up an audience', said Allison.

After a short break at New Year, 1958 got under way with a three-week tour, with a break in New York for the second *Ed Sullivan Show* performance, and a visit to a full-size studio, to finish recording for the *Buddy Holly* solo album. Of the tracks completed, only 'Rave On' was considered of a high enough standard for release, and the band left the studio to prepare themselves for a world tour starting in February.

They called first in Australia, where almost everything The Crickets had released was a hit. Supported by Paul Anka, who had scored a hit with 'Diana' and Jerry Lee Lewis, whose 'Great Balls Of Fire' was unstoppable, The Crickets were a guaranteed success. After a short tour of Florida, they were off for their one and only visit to Britain, where there was great excitement from fans who were giving The Crickets better chart placings than those in America. The single 'Listen To Me', which had not even been released in the States, got to number

16 in Britain. The British infatuation with all things American had shown itself the year before with the welcome given to Bill Haley and The Comets, and the rock 'n' roll message was clearly an American one in the style of British artists who took up the banner. Tommy Steele was an imitation of Gene Vincent, and the Elvis clones abounded, with Billy Fury, Marty Wilde, Rory Storm and, of course, Cliff Richard. Buddy's most overt imitator would be the Shadows' Hank Marvin, who took on the thick glasses and Fender guitar in a clear indication of where his influences lay.

The Crickets' four-week British tour got off to a disappointing start with a lacklustre performance on the television show *Sunday Night at the London Palladium* on 2 March. Buddy appeared with chewing gum over his teeth, because Joe Mauldin had accidentally knocked his caps off in a dressing-room mêlée. The other gigs were a great success, and saw The Crickets as part of a variety bill that included Des O'Conner, the 'comedian with the modern style', as the posters said. Reports of The Crickets' sets described them as 'the loudest show yet' and full of 'enthusiasm, drive and down-to-earth abandon'. The crowds were used, for the most part, to hearing live covers of their American heroes, and the fact that the well-rehearsed Crickets could play the songs just like the records accorded them an ecstatic reception. The band

Elvis Presley was an inspiration to
Buddy Holly

The clean-cut young star

were rewarded with increased record sales, 'Rave On' reaching number 5 in the charts following its release in April 1958 (in America it only got to number 37).

Back in America The Crickets leapt straight onto another tour package, coinciding with the release of *Buddy Holly*, whose sleeve picture showed Buddy without his glasses, looking quite unlike himself. The album contained a mixture of Holly originals and established covers, like 'You're So Square' and 'Ready Teddy' which had both been sung by Elvis. Neither *Buddy Holly* or *The 'Chirping' Crickets* made the charts during Buddy's lifetime, as The Crickets were very much a singles band, and the albums included the songs that had already sold so well as single releases.

Buddy's idea of a rest during a break in the tour was to put down a few more tracks with Petty. This session included the use of a piano, which featured on the best of the four completed songs, 'Think It Over'. It was the next single, and with its B-side, 'Fool's Paradise', also attracting attention, it reached number 11 in the American chart, number 27 in Britain. After the tour, Buddy played session man for a single released by Jerry Allison put out under his middle name, Ivan. 'Oh You Beautiful Doll/ Real Wild Child' was recorded as a bit of light relief, and is now a much sought-after rarity, as the lack of the

Holly/Crickets name gave a poor return on sales. Another session musician on the day was guitarist Tommy Allsup, with whom Buddy kept in touch for future sessions, as it was sometimes an advantage for him to have a competent guitarist so that he could concentrate on his vocal performance.

Two events of June 1958, on different trips to New York, put Buddy in the mood to change the organization of his career. Firstly, he recorded two songs at the Pythian Temple Studio without The Crickets or Norman Petty. It was Petty's idea to make use of the availability of two Bobby Darin compositions, 'Early in the Morning' and 'Now We're One', so it is doubtful that there was any bad feeling between Petty and Holly at the time of the sessions. However, Petty had been at the controls for all of Buddy's other releases, and Buddy's realization that other producers could create a winning sound must have given an amateur feel to the idea of the budget facilities at Clovis, in comparison to its New York alternative. 'Early in the Morning/Now We're One' was cut with session musicians and included Buddy's first use of the saxophone and a black gospel chorus group, and the occasion was an enjoyable and exciting one for him. The single wound up just outside the top 30 in America, but climbed to number 17 in Britain.

The scene of the crash

Ritchie Valens died with Buddy Holly

Secondly, Buddy met Maria Elena Santiago, a Puerto Rican working as a receptionist at Southern Music, The Crickets' music publisher. Buddy was immediately struck with the beautiful Maria, and after his business meeting he invited her out for lunch with the rest of the band. During the meal he announced that he was going to marry her, and asked her out on a date that evening, when she accepted his proposal. They had to overcome the protective nature of Maria's aunt, an executive in the Latin American division of Southern Music, who had looked after Maria since her mother had died when she was 8. There were worries from both families, one Baptist, the other Catholic, as religious discrimination was as much of a problem with many people as race. Any immediate problems were resolved by August 15, two months later, when Buddy and Maria were married in Lubbock by the local minister. They went on honeymoon in Acapulco with Jerry Allison and Peggy Sue, who had married just a few weeks before.

Buddy did not allow his married status to get in the way of his work, though, and he continued writing at his usual pace. He teamed up with Bob Montgomery once again during the summer of 1958, in the composition of two songs that they wanted the Everly Brothers to sing. They did full demos of 'Love's Made A Fool Of You' and 'Wishing' with session musicians, but the songs didn't get past Wesley Rose, the Everlys' manager, who wanted his artists' songs to remain in-house, for financial advantages. There was also a Crickets' session which resulted in the tracks 'It's So Easy', 'Lonesome Tears' and 'Heartbeat', a Latin-American influenced number that surely had Maria to thank for its genesis. In a rare moment of frivolity, the three Crickets all bought motorbikes, and relived some teenage days around the Lubbock streets.

In September Buddy was in the studio with King Curtis, the saxophone player from The Coasters, and Waylon Jennings, whom he had met as a DJ back in the Buddy and Bob days, and who was showing promise in country music. With Curtis, Mauldin and Allison, Buddy recorded 'Reminiscing', one of Curtis' songs, and 'Come Back Baby', an early song from Fred Neil, the writer of 'Everybody's Talkin' ', from the film *Midnight Cowboy*. Buddy kept Curtis on for the Jennings songs that he was to do production for, and although the single 'Jole Blon/When Sin Stops' was not successful, it showed Buddy's growing independence from Norman Petty.

His desire to work more for himself found him back at New York's Pythian Temple Studio in October, standing at the head of an orchestra. He had noticed a tendency towards softer rock 'n' roll in the charts, and wanted to try something new along those lines. With Dick Jacobs on production duties Buddy laid down 'True Love Ways', 'Moondreams', 'Raining In My Heart' and 'It Doesn't Matter Anymore', in a rock 'n' roll innovation equivalent to Charlie Parker's jazz session with strings of 1952.

'It Doesn't Matter Anymore' only just made it into the session, as Paul Anka had finished writing the song just hours before the recording was due to start. However it was well worth the last-minute rush, for Anka's songs were guaranteed to receive attention, even though he was only 18 at the time. It will never be known whether or not Buddy would have continued this sophisticated approach to his music; he could have gone on the road with an orchestral tour, as Charlie Parker did so successfully. What is sure is that he added a new slant to the possibilities of rock in what was to be his last studio session.

After the session Buddy rejoined The Crickets, now expanded with the addition of the session guitar skills of Tommy Allsup, who had been offered a place in the band; they had a television appearance and a short package tour with Eddie Cochran, Bobby Darin, Frankie Avalon and others. It was after the tour that Buddy decided to make the break with Norman Petty which his recent stabs at independence had been leading up to. He and Maria

The headlines break

Bobby Vee joined the Crickets after
Buddy's death

wanted to move to New York, which was the centre of the record industry, and the decision was a sensible career move. Maria's experience in the industry was a factor in his decision, and she would have been aware of services which Petty had not been delivering, such as professional advertising and publicity. Maria also made Buddy aware of Petty's unorthodox business methods. At the start of his management with The Crickets, he had persuaded Buddy that the Petty name on the writing credits would give more weight to their reception, as he already had a reputation. This had continued to some extent when Buddy's name was enough on its own; because of this it is unclear just how much input Petty had in the songwriting, although some songs, for example, 'Moondreams', were definitely Petty's.

Norman Petty had obviously been vital in the development of the Buddy Holly sound, and Buddy had been dependent on him from the very first session. Now he had shown that he could work successfully with another producer, as well as having his own production credits, so he decided to make the break, offering The Crickets the choice of moving to New York with him, or staying with Petty and Clovis. He made a new management agreement with Irving Fell, who was also Paul Anka's manager. Petty talked Allison and Mauldin into staying, and Buddy agreed that they should keep the Cricket name – quite a generous asset just to give away, as The Crickets had had more success than the solo Buddy Holly. Only Tommy Allsup took Buddy up on the move to New York and worked with him there.

Three Stars

For the last couple of months in 1958, Buddy acclimatized himself to his new life, setting up home and spending time with Maria, who had been forced to hide her married status in order not to upset Buddy's fans. Although he would not live long enough to follow many of his contemporaries into the world of film, the acting lessons that he took indicates that he might have had such a project in mind for the future. He did a little producing for his record company, and came up with the songs 'Peggy Sue Got Married' and 'Stay Close To Me'. 'Peggy Sue Got Married' was an evocative continuation of Buddy's original creation of the character, and the result of an idea of Buddy's father, and she would continue to be mentioned in songs of the period following Buddy's death.

Christmas 1958 was spent with Maria and the family in Lubbock, and followed a rather disappointing showing for the 'Heartbeat/Well . . . Alright' single. Buddy made a stop at the local radio station and staged a live impromptu rendition of 'You're the One' which he made up then and there, with just guitar and handclapping. The song would later be released with additional backing, and provides a light-hearted sketch of his effective yet simple technique.

Buddy entered the New Year of 1959 with a problem that should not have arisen for someone with his combination of success and quiet lifestyle: money. Norman Petty had been responsible for all The Crickets' financial dealings, and had control of the bank account. The band had always received money only through him, so by breaking up with him without first sorting out the situation, Buddy was leaving himself vulnerable to a financial stranglehold. As was his right as manager, Petty refused to let Buddy

Chip Epstein stars as Buddy in the musical
of his life

Maria with the band in later years

withdraw any money until their relationship had been officially wound up, and perhaps he was imagining that he could force Buddy to rejoin The Crickets. Rejecting that unthinkable notion, and with Maria's recent announcement that she was pregnant, the most obvious way to make ends meet was for Buddy to go on tour. Of several possible tours that he could join, he chose the 'Winter Dance Party' which would set off at the end of January.

In the time before the tour started, Buddy worked on a domestic tape recorder at home, doing half a dozen demos of new and recently written material, including 'Peggy Sue Got Married', 'Learning The Game' and

'Crying, Waiting, Hoping'. He started trying to organize a collaboration with R&B giant Ray Charles, who Buddy was hoping would do some producing with him. But Charles was on tour, and the project was put on hold. He formed a production company, Maria Music, which the new songs went onto, and he added to them six cover versions, including a Coasters' song, a Bo Diddley number and two versions of Little Richard's 'Slippin' And Slidin''. He also did a demo of the music hall song from 1906, 'Wait 'Till the Sun Shines Nellie', as a gift for his mother, though it would be part of the material collected for release after his death.

Despite having given The Crickets' name to Allison and Mauldin, Buddy borrowed it for the band he took on the 'Winter Dance Party': Tommy Allsup on guitar, Waylon Jennings on bass and the untried Charlie Bunch on drums. Maria's condition made it sensible for her to stay at home, and so, at the end of January 1959, the New Crickets joined Ritchie Valens, the Big Bopper, Frankie Sardo and Dion and The Belmonts on a coach that would have to brave the snow of the Mid-West winter. Ritchie Valens was a 17-year-old who had just had his first hit, 'Donna', and was publicizing its follow-up, 'La Bamba'. The Big Bopper (J. P. Richardson) was a DJ who had just scored a hit with 'Chantilly Lace', the more popular B-side to his novelty release 'The Purple People Eater Meets The Witch Doctor'. He was ready with his next single, 'Big Bopper's Wedding'. Buddy himself was hoping for a good reaction to the just-released 'It Doesn't Matter Anymore'.

The freezing winter weather brought immediate difficulties, with transport problems that left the party stuck in the snow, and Charlie Bunch had to receive hospital treatment for frostbite. By 2 February they were all tired and dirty, and Buddy decided to hire a plane to take him, Allsup and Jennings from the gig at Clear Lake, Iowa, to Moorhead, some 400 miles away. That would give him a

Rock 'n' rollers celebrate
Buddy Holly Week

Chip Epstein and Maria with the Crickets'
gold album

few desperately needed hours to sleep and put himself in a better frame of mind to go on stage that night. At short notice they chartered a plane from the Dwyer Flying Service, whose pilot, Roger Peterson, though inexperienced, was willing to take them to Moorhead's nearest airport in Fargo, North Dakota. Ritchie Valens and the Big Bopper learned of Buddy's plan and persuaded Allsup and Jennings to give up their places on the plane; they were suffering like the rest of the party, and Buddy's idea was one which any of them would have liked to take advantage of.

That evening's concert went down well in front of an audience of 1,100,

and the venue's manager chatted to
Buddy after the show, asking him of
his thoughts about the future. Buddy
is reported to have replied 'I'm either
going to the top – or I'm going to
fall. But I think you're going to see
me in the bigtime.' Buddy spoke to
Maria on the phone, telling her that
he was travelling ahead of the group
to organize things. Early in the
morning of 3 February, 1959, the
four-seater Beechcraft Bonanza took
off from the airport at Mason City.
Only a few minutes later it crashed
on a farm, ten miles away.

The demolished aircraft was discovered at 9.30 am by Jerry Dwyer, the
owner of the Dwyer Flying Service,
who flew over the route taken by the

plane, after he heard that it had not been reported as having landed at Fargo. The bodies of the singers had been thrown from the wreckage when the plane crashed into the snow – preventing any sound carrying to the farmhouse under half a mile away. The only imaginable reason for the crash was the appalling weather conditions, which would have meant Roger Peterson flying by instruments alone, a skill in which he was not practised. News travelled within hours of the discovery: Buddy's parents heard a report on the radio, as did Maria; she lost the baby soon after. The abysmal weather conditions prevented the transportation of the body for another day, and the funeral took place on 7 February at the Baptist Church in Lubbock. There were over a thousand people present to stand over the guitar-engraved head-stone, and messages came from all over the world, including one from Elvis Presley from his army unit in Germany. (In 1960, Elvis began to take long bus journeys, amid ru-mours of a recently developed fear of flying.)

The general shock at the tragedy was a factor in the success of 'It Doesn't Matter Anymore'; it rose to number 13 in the American charts, and shot to number 1 in 'Holly-mad' Britain. The 'Winter Dance Party' tour con-tinued, and auditions were organized in Moorhead to find replacements for the three dead artists. Robert Velline, known as Bobby Vee, impressed everyone with his rendition of some of Buddy's songs. Bobby Vee's future career would play on the memory of the man whose place he took, resulting in the 1964 album *I Remember Buddy Holly*. A tribute song, 'Three Stars' was recorded by several artists, most successfully by Eddie Cochran, though it was not released until after Cochran's death in a road accident in April 1960. The two luckiest members of the tour, Tommy Allsup and Waylon Jennings eventually got over the shock of the tragedy. Allsup would continue as a Cricket for some time, while Jennings made the most of his survival, with regular country hits during the 1960s. He was a major influence in the 'out-law country' style which gave Willie Nelson and Johnny Cash their most commercial success.

The Legend Lives On

Buddy's influence after his death affected the people who had worked with him as well as the public which had lapped up the few songs that he actually released. The primary source for the Buddy Holly industry was the songs and demos which had not been released before his death. These were in various stages of completion, from sketches of ideas that he had recorded at home, to full studio demos that would need only a polish to be ready for release. At first these were in the hands of producer Jack Hansen, who remastered the songs belonging to Maria Music. As a result, 'Peggy Sue Got Married' made number 13 in Britain in 1959, and an album, *The Buddy Holly Story Volume 2*, was released. However, it was obvious that Norman Petty was the man most experienced in recording the dead star, and he also had a lot of material from the Clovis sessions that he could work with. He collected as many of Buddy's tapes as he could find, and from 1962 he started to release the reworkings. He had ended his relationship with The Crickets and used a band called The Fireballs to play over those of Buddy's demos that needed attention. The results formed the albums *Reminiscing* (1963) and *Showcase* (1964). The order of the tracks takes no account of when they were written, probably because songs were chosen according to their quality as left by Buddy, but the comparison of old and new shows a uniformity of style from the early songs onwards. An aspect of the guaranteed success of additional material was that, by 1969, the well of Buddy's writing, which was in fact only 100 songs deep, was bringing up fairly muddy water. *Giant*, the album of that year, was completed with some of the sketchiest originals, and included songs which The Fireballs had already played over on previous releases. However, by presenting the public with new songs, the legend of Buddy Holly was kept alive, and even the early songs that he had written with Bob Montgomery, including 'I Wanna Play House With You' and 'Down The Line', found healthy sales on the 1965 album *Holly in the Hills*.

The Crickets themselves continued to play and record, with Sonny Curtis replacing Buddy at the front. Their commercial success, however, was not great, and the band went through several changes of personnel, with Jerry Allison the only constant member of the original line-up. They toured Britain during the 1960s and released a number of Buddy's songs, as well as their own material. And in a freak copy of Buddy's accident,

David Box, one of several singers in The Crickets, died in a plane crash in October 1964. In addition, influential British producer and Holly fan Joe Meek, who tried to contact Buddy through seances, committed suicide in a fit of depression on the anniversary of Buddy's death in 1967.

Buddy's wider influence is amazing, when it is considered that at his death he had only had seven songs in the American top 40, and a couple more in Britain. Looking beyond the songs which he had recorded, however, the welter of cover versions which have been made almost from the early 1960s right up to the present day guarantee a contemporary influence crossing most musical styles. The freshness and simplicity of his writing made him a basic palette onto which musicians could add their own colours, although many of them changed very little, not wanting to muddle the basic layers with the complications which modern technology makes so dangerously easy.

At the top of the hundreds of artists in obvious debt to him are The Beatles, whose insect name was itself a recognition of McCartney and Lennon's respect for The Crickets, while their cover of 'Words Of Love' differed very little from its original. According to Roy Orbison, The Beatles were 'just like Buddy Holly and The Crickets, but louder'. The Rolling Stones' version of 'Not Fade Away' was a marker in their movement away from the pure blues roots of their early days. Contemporaries of The Beatles and the Stones, like The Kinks and of course, The Hollies, carry Buddy's obvious influence in their music. Over 20 per cent of Buddy's songs have been recorded by other artists, many individual numbers have had several different treatments. 'That'll Be The Day' has been released by the Everly Brothers, Françoise Hardy, Pat Boone and Linda Ronstadt; 'Well . . . Alright' was covered by Bobby Sherman, Skeeter Davies, Blind Faith and Santana. Even the new wave of the late 1970s showed its debt to Buddy's talent, with Wreckless Eric's 'Crying,

Waiting, Hoping' and Blondie's 'I'm Gonna Love You Too'.

It is not surprising, seeing the publishing revenue to be gained from Buddy's music, that Paul McCartney went beyond his initial admiration during his time with The Beatles, and his work with Denny Laine on his album of Buddy's songs, *Holly Days*, by buying the rights to 90 per cent of the Buddy Holly catalogue in 1976. As a promotion for the acquisition, and, in recognition of the unending public interest in Buddy's legacy, an annual 'Buddy Holly Week' was set up in London around Buddy's birthdate in September. In 1977, the 1960 line-up of The Crickets, Jerry Allison, Joe Mauldin and Sonny Curtis reformed for that year's celebration. A Memorial Society was set up in America in 1978 in proof of the fact that, although America was behind Britain in its adulation of Buddy, he is an acknowledged legend in both countries, and his importance is unlikely to wane. As Bob Dylan said, 'The singers and musicians I grew up with transcend nostalgia – Buddy Holly and Johnny Ace are just as valid to me today as then'.

'That'll Be The Day' proved its importance as a symbol of rock 'n' roll's early years in the 1972 film which took its name from the song and recreated the era with a starring role from David Essex. In 1978, *The Buddy Holly Story* was released as a film, and the facts of his rise from a poor background and his death at the height of popularity made the sort of screenplay which usually has to be invented. Complaints that the film did not keep to the events of Buddy's life were not surprising, as both Norman Petty and The Crickets refused to allow themselves to be portrayed in it. *The Buddy Holly Story* went on to win an Oscar for Score Adaptation and a nomination for Best Actor for Gary Busey, who played Buddy. Busey was interested enough in the Holly myth to buy one of Buddy's acoustic guitars for $242,000 in 1990. In the same year as the film release, the compilation album *20 Golden Greats* was responsible for Buddy's topping the British album charts over 19 years after his death. A musical, *Buddy*, opened in London in 1989, and the production was staged all around the world, including a three-year touring show that covered Britain at the same time that the London production was running. It is estimated that over 8 million people have witnessed its continual revival of Buddy's memory.

The most abiding musical epitaph to the man who helped to set rock 'n' roll in its unconquered place at the top of modern popular music is to be found in the lyrics of singer Don McLean's 1972 song 'American Pie'. It reached number 1 in America and number 2 in Britain, and describes a freezing day in February as 'the day the music died'. It would be more accurate to say that although the tragedy of that morning took the life of Buddy Holly, the music is the element which has continued to live, more than three decades after his death. Any news concerning him always finds its way into the media, including one particularly poignant reminder, in February 1980. The police files at Mason City were being cleaned up, and the contents of one dusty-covered 20-year-old file were found to include, along with a watch that had belonged to the Big Bopper, an unmistakable pair of black-rimmed glasses.